DATE DUE			

SNAKES

～ SEYMOUR SIMON ～

HarperCollins*Publishers*

There are about twenty-five hundred different kinds of snakes in the world. Some people think all snakes are poisonous. But in fact, only a few hundred kinds are poisonous, and only about fifty of these are really dangerous to humans. Most snakes are harmless. Snakes stay away from people as much as they can.

Snakes live all over the world except for the Arctic and Antarctic, Iceland, Ireland, New Zealand, and a few small oceanic islands. Most snakes live on or under the ground; some live in trees, and a few others spend all or part of their lives in water. Snakes, such as this emerald tree boa, are often colorful, with a variety of beautiful patterns on their skins. Many behave in odd and unusual ways. Snakes are among the most interesting creatures on earth.

Snakes are reptiles and are related to lizards, turtles, alligators, and crocodiles. Like other reptiles, snakes have backbones and scaly skins, and are cold-blooded. That does not mean that they are cold, but that the temperature of a snake's body depends upon the temperature around it. Snakes need warm surroundings to be active. For this reason, most snakes are found in warm regions or are active mainly during warm weather.

A snake has no legs, and the thin body may be as short as your finger or as long as a school bus. A snake is not just a head attached to a long tail. Its tail starts after the anal opening on the underside of its body, and may be anywhere from a few inches to a third of its body length. The rest of a snake's body contains its heart, lungs, stomach, and other organs. The organs are long and thin, just like the body.

Humans have about thirty-two or thirty-three small bones, called vertebrae, that make up their backbones. But some large snakes have as many as five hundred vertebrae. Because of its many vertebrae, a snake, such as this poisonous island vine snake, can easily bend its body this way and that.

A snake is strong for its size. Pound for pound, snakes are among the strongest of animals. Even small snakes are muscular, because they have to push their way along the ground when they move.

Snakes can't walk or run, but they have at least three ways of moving. Most snakes loop along the ground—or other surface, such as a tree branch—to move forward. A snake draws its body into a series of curves and then suddenly straightens out. As each loop pushes backward against the surface, part of the snake moves forward. Snakes can move quickly this way, but most snakes can be easily outdistanced by a running person.

A kind of "squeeze-box" motion is used by some burrowing snakes. The snake coils itself together and throws the front end of its body forward. Then the snake anchors its front end along the sides of the burrow and pulls its tail forward. Snakes with thick bodies, such as boas, can also inch along the ground in a kind of caterpillar motion.

Still another kind of snake motion is called sidewinding. Some kinds of rattlesnakes and vipers use sidewinding to move across the loose, hot sands of a desert. This sidewinder arches the front end of its body and throws it to one side. Then it lifts the rest of its body high above the ground and loops it forward. The tracks of a sidewinder look like the rungs of a crooked ladder.

Snakes can also climb trees and swim.

Snakes keep growing all their lives. They grow much more quickly when they are young. Rattlesnakes may double in length by the end of the first year, and some pythons may even triple in length during that time. The rate of growth depends upon the kind of snake, the available food, the climate, and the individual. The rate of growth slows as snakes age, but may never stop completely even after a certain age as it does with humans and other mammals. An old snake of a long-lived kind will grow only a little bit, but it may still grow.

It is difficult to know how long snakes live in the wild. No one has ever observed a wild snake all of its life. But some kinds of snakes have lived in zoos for more than twenty years. So scientists assume that larger snakes, such as this ball python, may live for twenty to thirty years, and smaller snakes may live for ten to fifteen years.

All snakes eat animals. Usually, snakes do not chase after their prey. Either they lie quietly and blend into their surroundings until the prey comes close enough to be struck, or else they sneak up on it. Many snakes eat animals that humans consider pests, like rats and mice. No snake chews its prey. The snake opens its double-hinged jaws and spreads its elastic throat wide enough to swallow a whole animal that may even be much larger than the snake's head.

Almost any animal that is not too big can make a meal for a snake. Small snakes, such as this yellow rat snake, can eat insects, lizards, birds and their eggs, fish, and rodents. Larger snakes can also feed on rabbits, deer, monkeys, pigs, chickens, sheep, and goats. It may take a large snake hours to swallow a really big animal such as a pig or a goat, and weeks or even months before the snake needs another meal. The time depends upon the size and the shape of the prey.

Snakes have senses such as touch that help them find their prey and avoid danger. But their senses of sight, hearing, and smell are different from ours.

Most snakes probably do not see color and shape as well as humans do, but they can spot the slightest movement around them.

Snakes have inner ears rather than ears outside their bodies. Their internal ears make it difficult for snakes to hear sounds that travel through the air. But they can easily hear ground vibrations—even the quiet rustling of an approaching mouse.

Snakes also have an excellent sense of smell. A snake smells with its forked tongue as well as with its nose. The tongue picks up tiny particles of prey odors that float in the air or on the ground. Then the tongue carries the particles back to two small pits, called Jacobson's organs, in the roof of the mouth. Some snakes, such as this copperhead, have heat-sensing pits in front of their eyes so that they can track warm animals even at night.

Snakes are not slimy. A snake's skin is hard and smooth to allow the snake to slide easily over the ground. Its scales are thickened, hardened parts of the lower layers of skin. Snakes' eyes are covered by thin, transparent scales called spectacles. Usually the scales on a snake's head and its underside are larger than those on the rest of its body. A snake's skin is important to its survival. The colors and patterns of the skin may help to hide the snake among its surroundings, or they may serve to warn enemies away.

Snakes have three layers of skin. As the snake grows larger, it sheds its thin outer skin to make room for its growing body. The spectacles over the eyes are also shed, and the snake must grow new ones along with a new outer skin. Young, quickly growing snakes may shed six or more times a year. Body scales are sometimes strangely shaped, like the "horns" on the head of this eyelash viper.

Many kinds of snakes mate in the spring. Female snakes usually lay eggs in the early summer, one or two months after mating. Egg-laying snakes are called *oviparous* [oh-VIP-uh-rus] by scientists. Egg-laying species include pythons, hognoses, coral snakes, milk snakes, and king snakes.

Snakes lay their eggs in damp rotting wood, in holes in the ground, or in deserted animal burrows. This green tree python's eggs are long and narrow and protected by a tough, leathery covering. While python mothers coil about their eggs and remain with them for two months or longer until they hatch, king snake eggs are left to hatch on their own, warmed by the sun. Untended snake eggs take anywhere from a few days to several weeks to hatch. A baby snake has an egg tooth to help it cut through the shell. Once they are laid, the quicker the eggs hatch the better. Unhatched eggs may be eaten by animals that chance upon them.

Garter snakes, boas, water snakes, and pit vipers keep their developing eggs within their own bodies until the eggs hatch. Then they bear living young. Live-bearing snakes are called *ovoviviparous* [oh-voh-vy-VIP-uh-rus]. Young snakes are on their own; no snakes take care of their babies.

After they hatch, snakes have many enemies waiting to snap them up for a meal. Baby snakes are killed and eaten by frogs, pigs, skunks, hedgehogs, opossums, badgers, foxes, coyotes, and many other animals. Each of these animals has its own method of hunting. Some animals, such as mongooses, have the quickness to bite and kill even poisonous cobras. Birds such as eagles, hawks, road runners, and secretary birds regularly prey upon snakes. An eagle or a hawk will plunge down from the sky and grip a snake with its claws before the snake can defend itself. The bird then kills the snake with its sharp beak. Long-legged birds such as secretary birds and road runners regularly hunt and kill snakes.

Some snakes eat other snakes. King snakes and racers regularly feed upon smaller snakes. This king snake is swallowing a young rattlesnake. Humans are probably the biggest threat to snakes, because they often destroy the wild places that snakes need to live. Humans also rarely miss a chance to kill a rattler. Some people will unreasonably kill any kind of snake, even if it is harmless and poses no danger.

About three quarters of all the snakes in the world are generally harmless snakes that belong to a family called *Colubridae*. Among the colubrids are garter snakes, water snakes, rat snakes, grass snakes, milk snakes, and racers. None of these snakes is very large; each has a different way of protecting itself. Some have skin colors and patterns that blend in with their surroundings and make the snakes difficult to see. Other kinds of snakes hiss at an enemy or rear up in a threatening way. Some also flatten their bodies, which makes them look larger and more dangerous than they really are.

The most unusual defensive behavior among these harmless snakes is that of the hognoses. These snakes get their name from their upturned snout, which, like a hog's nose, is used for digging in the ground. When you startle a hognose, it puffs out its head and body and sways back and forth like a miniature cobra. Come too close, and the hognose will hiss loudly and open its jaws wide. But the hognose will not bite. If it is still being bothered after its fearsome display, the hognose will suddenly roll over on its back. It looks as if the snake is really dead. But if you flip the hognose right side up, the "dead" snake will immediately flip over on its back again, and it will remain that way until the danger has passed.

The biggest snakes are the longest land animals that are alive today—longer than an elephant or a giraffe. These giant snakes use their long, flexible bodies to throw coils around their prey. The slowly tightening coils do not crush the prey's body to pulp. Instead, the prey cannot breathe and dies of suffocation in a few minutes.

Giant snakes sometimes attack people, but they almost never try to eat them. One reason is that most humans are just too large and too quick to be caught easily. Another reason is that humans are smart and in a group can help one another fend off the snake. If a giant snake does attack a person, it is probably because the snake mistakes the person for an animal that it normally preys upon. A person is more likely to be hit by lightning than attacked by a giant snake.

All the giant snakes are either boas or pythons and belong to the *Boidae* family. (Not all boas and pythons are giants; there are many smaller kinds.) If you take length, thickness, and heaviness into account, the anaconda (a boa) is the biggest snake in the world. There are a number of reports of anacondas in the wild that measured over thirty feet long. Anacondas live in swamps and on the banks of lakes and rivers in tropical parts of South America, where this one was photographed.

Most of the poisonous snakes in the United States belong to a family called *Viperidae*, or vipers. Vipers have large poison glands in their heads, connected by ducts to long, curved poison fangs in the front of the upper jaws. When not in use, the fangs fold back and lie flat. When a viper is ready to bite, the fangs spring forward and become erect.

The viper family is made up of two large subfamilies: true vipers and pit vipers. True vipers live mostly in Africa, with a few kinds in Europe and Asia. True vipers include the Gaboon viper, the puff adder, and the European adder, the only poisonous snake in England.

Pit vipers, so named because of the heat-sensing pits on their heads, live mostly in the Americas and include about twenty kinds of rattlesnakes, the water moccasin or cottonmouth, and the copperhead. Rattlesnakes, such as this diamond-back, live mainly in the southwestern United States and northwest Mexico, but some rattlers are found in every other mainland state except Maine and Delaware. The rattle is made up of special interlocking scales at the end of the snake's tail. When the tail is shaken, the rattles hit against each other and make a noise like a buzzing insect. The rattle often frightens away enemies.

Cobras, mambas, coral snakes, the taipan, and the death adder belong to another family of poisonous snakes, called *Elapidae*. Elapids are found mostly in Asia, Africa, Australia, and South America, though coral snakes are found from Florida north to the Carolinas and west to Texas. Elapid snakes have fixed, hollow poison fangs that are always erect and ready for use.

The king cobra is the largest of all poisonous snakes, sometimes reaching a length of more than fifteen feet. The Indian cobra, shown here, is also known as the spectacled cobra because of the eyelike markings on its hood. It raises its hood by pushing forward the long ribs behind its neck. Because the Indian cobra is commonly found in populated areas of India and southeast Asia, it is far more likely to bite a person than is the rarer king cobra.

Australia is the only continent with more poisonous than nonpoisonous kinds of snakes. Two of the most deadly are the death adder and the taipan. The bite of a death adder is often fatal. The taipan is a large snake that grows to more than ten feet. A person bitten by this snake will probably die within a few minutes. The only reason the taipan doesn't kill many people is that it is scarce and will usually try to escape rather than attack.

Even though only about fifty kinds of poisonous snakes are really dangerous to humans, they are more deadly than lions, tigers, wolves, bears, and sharks all put together. Poisonous snakes kill more people in a single year than all these animals do in one hundred years; they kill more people in a single *day* than killer whales have ever done in all of history. India has the highest number of fatal snakebites—between ten and twenty *thousand* deaths each year. In the United States there are about one dozen deaths a year from snakebites.

Of course, poisonous snakes that come into houses, farms, or towns must be destroyed. But snakes, including poisonous kinds, such as this golden eyelash viper, play an important role in nature by keeping down the rodent population that eats crops and carries disease. If all snakes were to disappear, rodents would increase greatly, crops would be destroyed, and there might be more human suffering because of lack of food or the spread of disease than snakes could ever cause.

Snakes behave in some ways that we like and in other ways that we don't like. But that is true of almost every animal in the world. To appreciate the special qualities of snakes is to appreciate the diversity of all life.

Library of Congress Cataloging-in-Publication Data
Simon, Seymour.
    Snakes / by Seymour Simon.
       p.   cm.
    Summary: Describes, in text and photographs, the physical
characteristics, habits, and natural environment of various species
of snakes.
       ISBN 0-06-022529-7. — ISBN 0-06-022530-0 (lib. bdg.)
       1. Snakes—Juvenile literature. [1. Snakes.] I. Title.
QL666.O6S456 1992   91-15948
597.96—dc20   CIP
                                                     AC

PHOTO CREDITS:

Jacket and pp. 5, 9, 18, 32 © K.H. Switak;
pp. 2-3, 6, 10, 14, 17, 25, 31 © Jim Bridges;
pp. 13, 21, 23, 26 © J. Cancalosi;
p. 29 © Alan & Sandy Carey.

JACKET:

A green tree python hatches either yellow
or brown and then turns green as an adult.

PAGES 2-3:

Florida kingsnake eggs hatching

PAGE 32:

The South African boomslang is a poisonous
snake that lives in trees.